CONTENTS

KU-167-167

WELCOME

TO THE

THE ULTIMATE GUIDE TO

STRANGER THINGS

★ ♫

Explore the mysterious and captivating world of the hit Netflix series. With its mix of sci-fi, horror, and coming-of-age drama, *Stranger Things* has captured the hearts of fans around the world. From the fictional small town of Hawkins, Indiana, to the eerie Upside Down, it's taken us on a wild ride full of thrills, chills, and 80s nostalgia.

HELLFIRE CLUB

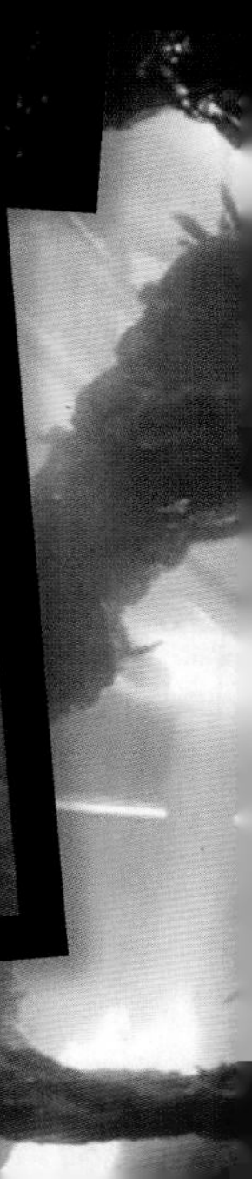

One of the most beloved aspects of *Stranger Things* is its cast of characters, each with their own unique strengths and vulnerabilities. From the determined and fiercely loyal Eleven to the lovable goofball Dustin, there's someone for everyone to root for. Our character profiles bring you the backstories and motivations of each of the main players.

Of course, *Stranger Things* wouldn't be complete without its iconic moments and thrilling plotlines. We'll highlight some of the most memorable scenes from the series, from the spine-tingling first encounter with the Demogorgon to the epic battles against the Mind Flayer and Vecna. Relive the joys and heartbreaks of each season, and get ready for Season 5 with exclusive insights and predictions about what might happen next.

But *Stranger Things* isn't just about the characters and storylines; it's also a celebration of 80s pop culture. From the synth-heavy soundtrack to the retro fashion, the series is steeped in nostalgia. We'll bring you a closer look at the classic rock hits that feature throughout the show. We'll also explore the fashion of Hawkins, from Eleven's iconic jumpsuit to Hopper's flowery shirt obsession.

INDIANA HAWKINS

SO JOIN US ON A JOURNEY INTO THE UPSIDE DOWN, AS WE EXPLORE THE WORLD OF *STRANGER THINGS* AND CELEBRATE THE ENDURING LEGACY OF THIS UNFORGETTABLE SERIES.

SEASON 1 BEST BITS

Let's face it, when we all started watching Season 1, we had no idea just HOW AMAZING *Stranger Things* was going to be. Let's look back at some of the OMG moments from that epic first season.

AND SO IT BEGINS...

Talk about throwing you in at the deep end! In the first two minutes, we see something scary escape from a lab (RIP white coat science dude), then poor Mike gets chased home from a Dungeons & Dragons night before hiding in the shed. It's edge-of-the-seat stuff but somehow, the light glowing brighter and Mike disappearing is scarier than any monster bursting in!

XMAS LIGHTS

The moment that Joyce realises that Will can communicate through the lights is IMMENSE. Not sure how happy her landlord would be with her painting the alphabet on the wall to help him spell out his answers, mind you. And whose blood DIDN'T run cold when he spelt out R.....U....N. Eek!

MEETING ELEVEN

Wandering barefoot through the woods isn't the standard way to introduce a legend, but what is standard about El? Wearing a hospital gown and sporting a shaved head, she's obviously escaped from somewhere but we don't know where!

She finds Benny's Diner and hey, even kids with ESP need fries and a greasy burger from time to time. She sneaks in and gets caught helping herself, but Barney soon realises something is wrong. Instead of calling the police, the kindly chef feeds her up – but ew, El, table manners next time!

So far, so normal (ish). But this is El. A whirring fan in the corner of the room is annoying her, so she stops it with her mind. Like you do.

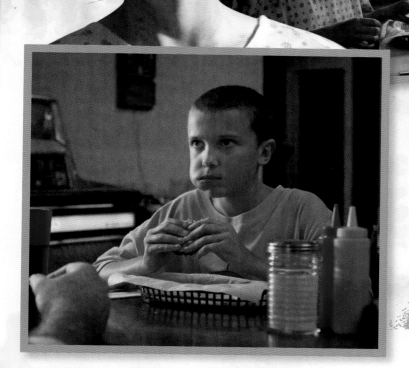

BYE TO BARB

If you will sneak around in bushes taking photographs of people who don't even know you are there (bit creepy, Jonathan) then there's always the chance you'll stumble across something scary. Sick of playing gooseberry to Steve and Nancy, Barb decides to sits alone by the pool at Steve's house, but the thing is she is not alone and is taken too. When will this madness end?

THE ULTIMATE SACRIFICE

'Goodbye Mike'. Two words. Absolute feels. The scene where the Demogorgon bursts into the classroom where Mike, El, Dustin and Lucas are holed up is totes terrifying even before El lifts herself off the table and tells the monster 'no more'. Calm as you like. A quick look back and 'Goodbye Mike', and the next thing you know she's sacrificed herself for those she loves. Time for a lie down in a darkened room after watching that.

AIN'T NOBODY

Something about Mike's body isn't adding up for Hop, so he sneaks back to the morgue ('I left my hat behind!') and knocks out the guard (well, a Hop's gotta do what a Hop's gotta do). As soon he gets hands on with Will's 'body' it's clear something's not right – it's stuffed with more cotton wool than a fairground teddy bear! WHAT THE HELL?!?!

LEAP OF FAITH

We all know not to mess with El, right? Seems not everyone does. A couple of bullies pick on Dustin and Mike, making Mike jump off the cliff edge at Sattler Quarry to save Dustin from some amateur dental work. Just when it looks like Mike is about to lose ALL his HP, El levitates him the hell out of there – then beats up the bullies with her mind. The word you are looking for is epic.

WILL'S RESCUE

Hands up, who would wander into the Upside Down with just a hazmat suit for protection. Yeah, us neither. But we're not Joyce and Hop, who find Will, bring him back from Upside Down and resuscitate him. Heroic.

TURN TO **PAGE 18** FOR
SEASON 2 BEST BITS

ELEVEN

When we first meet El, as she stumbles out of the woods barefoot and wearing only a hospital gown, it's clear that something very unusual has happened to her. Be honest though, none of us could have predicted just HOW unusual El's life had been.

Taken from her mother the moment she was born and used by Dr Brenner to try and open a portal to another dimension (which we now know as the Upside Down), El's story throughout *Stranger Things* is about her growing up and experiencing things that other kids her own age had taken for granted.

Of course, she isn't like other kids (although she does lose her powers for a while which looked like it was going to give her a chance at normality!) and El has to balance her extraordinary powers with the love she develops for her new friends and family. IT makes her a loyal, brave ally to the group.

> "I KEPT THE DOOR OPEN THREE INCHES. I NEVER STOPPED BELIEVING."

EL AND HOPPER

Before she escaped from Hawkins National Laboratory, the closest thing El had to a father figure was Dr Brenner, the man she called Papa. That villain was nothing like a father, of course, but El soon finds a man she could consider a dad – Jim Hopper. Like any father/daughter relationship they fight like cat and dog, but their love for each other is next level. You only have to listen to Hopper reading his letter out after his 'death' and you'll be blubbing.

EL AND EIGHT

The way El was brought up may mean she was away from her blood family – but she did make good friends with one of the other children to be part of Brenner's twisted take on scientific research. Eight and Eleven became close during their time in the lab, so it's great to see them meet up when El travels to Chicago in Season 2. Eight (aka Kali) even teaches El how to control her powers better!

EL JUST WANTS TO HAVE FUN

After an incredibly limited childhood where all she really saw was the inside of a laboratory, El is finally able to discover that she has a fun side. She's a goofy, fun-loving kid at heart and her friendship with Max really brings that side of her out more and more – their shopping trip to Starcourt Mall is absolutely iconic!

EL'S DIET

It's easy to forget that El is just a little girl at heart, but you get reminded of that real quick when you see what she eats! She's not one for making sure she gets her five a day, that's for sure. Eggos (of course), French toast, TV dinners with Hopper, ice cream – you name it, whatever she eats is bound to be unhealthy.

EL THE BRAVE!

El is incredibly brave and loyal and is never afraid to put herself in danger if it means protecting her friends. She demonstrates this over and over, frequently fighting monsters – and even risking her life – for those she loves. That's what friends are for.

THE GATE. I OPENED IT. I'M THE MONSTER.

JIM HOPPER

From the moment we first meet Hopper, you just know he's a committed, dedicated, hardworking policeman who believes that the role of the police is a crucial one.

Ha, not really and we all know it! He's a jaded, cynical, washed up copper whose heart really isn't in it after the death of his daughter and then his divorce. HOWEVER, the search for Will and then looking after Eleven proves to be the making of the man! Hopper rediscovers his passion and his principles, becoming the kind of Chief of Police that ANY town would be proud of, and (just maybe) the kind of man Joyce could fall for.

> BUT PLEASE, IF YOU DON'T MIND, FOR THE SAKE OF YOUR POOR OLD DAD, KEEP THE DOOR OPEN THREE INCHES.

HOPPER THE HERO

Nothing shows how big the change in Hopper is more than his awesome bravery at the end of Season 3. Knowing that the only way to kill the Mind Flayer would kill him too? Man, that took serious guts!

I'VE BEEN EXPECTING YOU

HOW LONG did it take for Hopper to finally plant a kiss on Joyce? Pretty much everyone spent three seasons screaming at the TV for them to get together – HOW much tension was there? We finally got our wish, but it took til Season 4 for them to realise what the rest of us had known all along – they were made for each other!

MEET
JOYCE BYERS

Joyce is pretty much everything a good mum should be. Sure, she's a little on the kooky side, but what's always super clear is the big love she has for her kids.

Right off the bat, she wouldn't give up on Will when he went missing, even though everyone thought she was nuts for thinking the house's electrics were talking to her. But, like mums nearly always are, she was right! Joyce's journey is a pretty epic one – from timid, jumpy mum to a fiercely protective monster-slaying warrior. Absolute badass.

PUZZLE MISTRESS

Joyce solves puzzles like a boss. She is definitely the brains of the operation and without her quick thinking and her ability to piece things together then Will would never have escaped the Upside Down in the first place. The way she figured out a way for him to talk by painting letters next to Christmas lights was epic – as was the way she pieced together what looked like random scribbles to reveal a map of the Upside Down!

MAYBE I AM A MESS!
MAYBE I'M CRAZY!
MAYBE I'M OUT OF MY MIND!

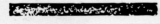

UNLUCKY IN LOVE?

Joyce hasn't had the best of luck with her love life! She's divorced from the boys' dad Lonnie (who is a pants dad as well as a pants husband) and then her new boyfriend Bob Newby was mauled to death by Demodogs inside the Hawkins lab! Let's hope she has more luck with Hop!

ELEVEN'S Waffle RECIPE

Eleven is totally obsessed with Eggos – but what are they, and how can you make them yourself?

MAKE YOUR OWN

WHAT YOU NEED

250 g plain flour

4 tsp of baking powder

2 tbsp of caster sugar

1 tsp of salt

2 eggs

375 ml of warm milk

75 g of butter

1 tsp of vanilla extract

A waffle maker (though you can make these as pancakes on the hob if you don't have one!)

Eggos are a brand of frozen waffles made by Kellogg's. However, they aren't available in the UK (though if you look in the freezer section of most supermarkets, you will find other brands sell frozen waffles).

INSTRUCTIONS:

First things first! Ask an adult to help, especially if you're going to be making pancakes rather than using a waffle maker.

STEP 1
In a bowl, beat the eggs and add the milk, butter and vanilla extract.

STEP 2
Now mix in the flour, baking powder, sugar and salt.

STEP 3
Make sure the mixture is well beaten and not lumpy.

SERVING SUGGESTIONS:

You can put fruit, ice cream, chocolate sauce, syrup, honey, butter or jam on your waffle! Whatever takes your fancy!

STEP 4
If you're using a waffle maker, heat it up and pour in the amount of mixture suggested by the manufacturer.

OR...
If you're making pancakes, heat your frying pan and wipe it (carefully) with some kitchen roll with a touch of sunflower oil on it, then pour in enough mixture to cover the surface area of the pan. Cook it for a minute or so on one side, until it is solid, then use a spatula to flip it over and cook the other side.

STRANGELY TRUE OR STRANGELY FALSE!

Think you know *Stranger Things* like the back of your hand? Time to put your knowledge to the test with our True or False Quiz!

1

Dustin has a pet turtle called Yertle.
TRUE ○ FALSE ○

2 
El' was named after the laboratory room number where she was experimented on.
TRUE ○ FALSE ○

3

Hawkins High basketball team is nicknamed 'The Lions'
TRUE ○ FALSE ○

4 
CHAPTER ONE
THE VANISHING OF WILL BYERS
Season 1 of *Stranger Things* starts in 1983.
TRUE ○ FALSE ○

5 
Max and Billy moved to Hawkins from New York State.
TRUE ○ FALSE ○

6

LEAVING HAWKINS COME AGAIN SOON
The town of Hawkins, Indiana is a real place.
TRUE ○ FALSE ○

7 Jim Hopper had a son with his ex-wife.

TRUE ◯ FALSE ◯

8 Robin Buckley can speak four different languages.

TRUE ◯ FALSE ◯

9 When he is not the Dungeon Master, Will plays D&D as a Paladin.

TRUE ◯ FALSE ◯

10 Lucas' little sister is called Elena.

TRUE ◯ FALSE ◯

11 Eleven loves Eggos and frozen waffles.

TRUE ◯ FALSE ◯

12 In Season 1, Barb is the first person to disappear.

TRUE ◯ FALSE ◯

13 Hopper was in the US Army during the Vietnam conflict.

TRUE ◯ FALSE ◯

14 In Season 2, Joyce's boyfriend Bob was the manager at the local branch of Blockbuster Video.

TRUE ◯ FALSE ◯

ANSWERS ON PAGE 78

SEASON 2 BEST BITS

We thought *Stranger Things* couldn't get any better after Season 1 blew our collective minds. How wrong we were – here's a look at some of the moments and scenes that defined Season 2.

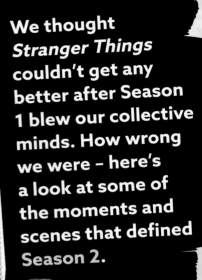

THERE ARE OTHERS

Season 2 roared onto our screens with a high-octane car chase as a group of hoodlums flee the police after a heist. They're able to escape when the police see an illusion, believing a collapsing bridge is stopping them from continuing the chase. Making them see that would surely take some kind of ESP, and it's only when one of the girls in the van rolls up her sleeve to show a tattoo of the number 8 that we realise – El is not the only one to have escaped Hawkins National Laboratory...

BOB THE BRAVE

Men don't come more decent than Bob Newby. The way he took Joyce and her boys into his heart was so touching, and at the end of it all, Bob showed just how much he loved them all. With the Byers trapped by the Demodogs, Bob used his technical skills to disable the security systems and lead them to safety. Sadly, he didn't get to join them, and was killed by a Demodog in front of a horrified Joyce.

DON'T STROKE IT, DUSTIN!

Everyone loves a tale about a young boy that adopts an abandoned pet and nurses it back to full health as they bond, right? Not when it's a baby Demodog (a Demopuppy?) they don't. Exactly what Dustin was thinking is a mystery. As D'artagnan (or Dart) grows, we could all see where this was going way before Dusty did.

MAX STANDS UP TO BILLY

Max and Billy have a troubled relationship as step-siblings. Billy's bullying of Max is a recurrent theme in their relationship, as is the way he treats the world in general with a lack of respect. In this scene, Max has had enough, knocking Billy out with a jab before threatening him with a spiked basedball bat. Gulp!

I LOVE THIS TOWN!

This scene is about so much more than the reference to the (amazing) *Ghostbusters* film. The way that Mike assumed that Lucas would be Winston just because they were both black is naïve rather than nasty, but Lucas teaches us all a lesson as he points out that Venkmann was far cooler and he want to be the cool guy too. And the outfits totally rock!

THE SNOW BALL

After the intense and frankly terrifying storyline of Season 2, the Snow Ball is a welcome way to wrap things up. The Hawkins Middle School ball is a chance for all the lead characters to come together and forget their worries for a night. The music – 'Time after Time' by Cyndi Lauper and 'Every Breath You Take' by The Police is perfect. We even get a couple of first smooches, as both Mike and Eleven and Max and Lucas are swept along by the moment. Oh – and Dustin's hair deserves some kind of award all of its own.

LOOK WHO'S BACK!

With the gang under siege from a demodog in their hiding place at the Byers' house, all looks lost. From out of nowhere, they hear what sounds like the demodog taking a serious beating before its lifeless body smashes through the window. Of course it's El, who unlocks the door with her mind and walks in looking cooler than ever. Great time to pop back, El!

BORN AGAIN

After meeting her mother but being unable to get any sense out of her, Eleven uses her powers to access her own mother's memories. That results in a flashback sequence that sees El looking on horrified as she is born, then seeing Dr Brenner tell her family that she hadn't made it – when she was fine all along. It's another insight into Brenner's total lack of morals.

WAR OF INDEPENDENCE

El's relationship with Hopper is not always the easiest, and Season 2 shows the difficulties they have as El gets older and becomes much more independent. Hopper wants to keep her safe from a world that could cause her so much harm – but Hop wouldn't be Hop if he didn't get it completely wrong from time to time. Their fight in Season 2 is soooo relatable – El's frustrations with his over-protection boil over and they really go at each other. She even compares him to Brenner – 'You're just like Papa'...ouch!

CLOSE THE GATE

Not a scene for the faint-hearted, this one has everything. El stands magnificent in the ruins of Hawkins National Laboratory, and begins to close the gate to the Upside Down so no more evil creatures can make it through to our dimension. The Mind Flayer isn't having any of that though, and there's a huge battle between the two. With an almost superhuman effort, El uses the last of her power to close the gate, causing her to collapse in exhaustion as a huge explosion rips through the area. Intense.

TURN TO **PAGE 34** FOR
SEASON 3 BEST BITS

MIKE WHEELER

The boss, the head honcho, the numero uno. However you say it, there's no doubt that Mike is the leader of the gang.

He's the glue that holds them all together, and is just that guy that people look to when no-one knows what they should do next. He might not be the smartest, the strongest or the fastest of the group – but he's totally the one that makes all the big decisions. However, as the group grow up, Mike ends up with all his focus on his relationship with El. He's even rude to Will – unthinkable in the first couple of seasons. It's all part of growing up, but we hope he's back on better form by Season 5 as he's at his best when he's part of the gang, not falling out with people.

IF ANYONE ASKS WHERE I AM, I'VE LEFT THE COUNTRY.

FRIENDS TILL THE END

Do you want to know what friendship really looks like? When Dustin is being bullied, Mike steps off a cliff to save his friend from a beating. Sure, El turns up in the nick of time to save him, but Mike had no way of knowing that would happen – so his actions really were super brave (ok, ok, and maybe a bit mad!)

THE THREE INCH RULE

Everyone wants a bit of privacy when they start dating, but poor Mike doesn't get much of that when El inevitably falls for his strong looks and even stronger leadership skills. Let's just say Hop isn't the most chilled of dads. *'THREE INCH RULE! NO MAKING OUT!'* Give them a break, Hop! Mike's a respectful guy!

kiss me

MEET

WILL BYERS

Will is the boy that started off this whole crazy adventure – though he wasn't too keen on the idea at the time!

When he was abducted and taken to the Upside Down, things started to unravel real fast. He's an unlikely hero, being a shy, quiet and caring kid, but don't let that fool you. What Will went through in the Upside Down and then being possessed would freak most adults out, let alone a kid. Will though? He never gave up. That quiet determination is clearly genetic – never mess with a Byers, y'all hear?

ROLL THE DICE!

Will's the name, Dungeons & Dragons is the game! Though all the boys love D&D, Will is the one they look to as Dungeon Master (DM). Think about it – it's a role that needs imagination, courage and calmness. Who better than Will for that role?! He's not nicknamed Will the Wise for nothing!

> **WHEN YOU'RE DIFFERENT, SOMETIMES YOU FEEL LIKE A MISTAKE.**

READY OR NOT?

You don't need to be big and strong to be a hero – it's all about attitude. When Will was in the Upside Down, he survived by using his small size to his advantage, hiding from the Mind Flayer and staying alive in the process. His brother Jonathan did say Will was basically a hide and seek champion – he wasn't kidding!

MEET

DUSTIN HENDERSON

Every group of friends needs a tech guy – and boy does Dustin tick every box when it comes to that title!

He loves taking things apart, figuring out how they work, and learning how to make them himself. His expertise with radio and communications systems in general is a really important part of the gang's adventures, making sure they can talk to each other and stay safe. Aside from that, Dustin's geekiness and his awkwardness around girls is funny and cute at the same time – he's always completely awks even though he thinks he's acting chill. One thing's for sure though – this is a guy with a heart of gold who will always do anything for his friends.

WE NEVER WOULD'VE UPSET YOU IF WE KNEW YOU HAD SUPERPOWERS.

NEVER ENDING... EMBARRASMENT

So at some point in your life, you're probably going to have a partner who makes you do embarrassing stuff. Whether it's a cutesy nickname, or pulling a cute face, a silly voice or whatever, the key is – KEEP IT SECRET. Poor Dustin doesn't get that luxury from Suzie though, and has to sing 'The NeverEnding Story' to her. In front of all his mates.

BROMANCE

Dustin is useless with girls, but his friendship with Steve is definitely one of the sweetest themes in *Stranger Things*. They couldn't be more different in SO MANY ways, but they are absolutely tight –developing their own handshake, swapping hair tips, ohh yeah and saving THE ENTIRE UNIVERSE together.

MEET

LUCAS SINCLAIR

Lucas is a deep thinker who always wants to know what the reasons are behind a decision, and what's in it for other people.

Sometimes this can make him seem a bit rude and unfriendly, but he only does it because he loves his friends so much that he doesn't want to see any of them get hurt. His suspicious approach to welcoming Eleven into the friendship circle is a good example of that – he just takes a little longer to develop enough trust to let her in. Once you're on team Lucas, however, he'll go to the ends of the earth for you – it can just take a while!

BALLER OR HELLFIRE?

In Season 4, Lucas finds himself in a bit of a dilemma after he joins the basketball team. On the one hand, he can now be one of the 'cool kids' but on the other, he feels like he is selling out his old buddies in the Hellfire Club. It's a hard decision to make, the poor guy!

> ## FRIENDS DON'T LIE. NEVER EVER. NO MATTER WHAT.

QUICK-THINKING LUCAS!

Lucas is probably the most inventive of the group. Maybe it's his love of science that helps him work round a problem – who knows? One thing's for sure though – he uses whatever is at hand to defeat his enemies. In Season 1 he defeats a Demogorgon by using a slingshot, and in Season 3 he beats the Mind Flayer with fireworks!

MEET
MR CLARKE

If all schoolteachers were as cool as Mr Clarke, we'd all get better grades. He's that rarest of things, a Science teacher that actually gets his students and wants to make his classes as fun as possible. He enjoys his job so much that he helps the boys outside school hours too. He gives them access to the Heathkit radio set, teaches them about alternate dimensions, tells them how to make a sensory deprivation tank and even helps Joyce understand what's happening with her magnets. That's how teaching is done!

BARB HOLLAND

Barb is in *Stranger Things* for the shortest time, but made a real impact! While the whole of Hawkins loses its mind when Will goes missing, Barb barely gets a mention! All this despite being a great friend to Nancy and an all-round sound lady. She doesn't even get a funeral 'til Season 2 – no wonder #justiceforbarb was trending on social media at the time. We see you, Barb. We see you.

EIGHT

Stands to reason that if El's number 11, there must be at least ten others like her, right? Well, at the start of Season 2 we meet Eight – also known as Kali Prasad. We met her using her powers to help a gang pull off heists but working a side hustle in tracking down former Hawkins Lab associates. She's got a darker side to her than El, and is more manipulative – but the two have a shared past that ties them like nothing else can.

BOB NEWBY

Poor Bob was a one season wonder, meeting Joyce in Season 2 and becoming her boyfriend. He was a kind and caring guy who really took the whole family in, showing his love to both Will and Jonathan too. It was all looking great until the Byers were attacked by Demodogs. Bob used his electronics skills to disable the security system (all RadioShack employees are fully trained in how to do this) but as they made their escape, lovely Bob was mauled to death in front of a horrified Joyce. RIP Bob. You were a good man.

THE WHEELERS

The Wheeler family consists of dad Ted, mum Karen, and children Nancy, Mike and Holly. They're a pretty typical family living in a pretty unusual town and trying to make sense of the chaos around them. Ted never seems to quite know where he is, while Karen is one of those wonderfully clueless mums who thinks her kids are having a sleepover when in reality they are battling demons to save the future of humanity.

ERICA SINCLAIR

Erica is Lucas' little sister and starts out almost as a comedy character, pestering Steve and Robin in Scoops Ahoy for the free ice cream samples. However, she soon proves an invaluable ally as she's the only person small enough to climb into the vents in Starcourt Mall to explore the Russian base beneath it. Throughout the series she grows from being a bratty little sister to a fully-fledged nerd in her own right – including, of course, becoming a kick-ass D&D player herself!

SEASON 1&2
WHERE IT HAPPENED

THE BYERS' HOUSE

The home of the Byers family is not much to look at but is key to a lot of the action in the first two seasons. It's there that Will manages to communicate with Joyce through the Christmas lights for the first time. That same lounge is also where Joyce begins to piece together Will's drawings to show the maze of vines underneath Hawkins. The garden does, however, have a handy shed - though it turns out it's not much good for hiding from monsters.

CASTLE BYERS

Castle Byers is Will's very cool little hideaway in the nearby woods, a place he goes to read his comic books and just get some valuable me-time. Admittedly the 'castle' element of the name is a little on the grand side, but to Will it really is his castle - he hides there while in the Upside Down to stay safe. Just don't forget the secret password: Radagast.

HAWKINS NATIONAL LABORATORY

The home of unspeakable evil, both above and below ground. The lab is where El grew up, in sterile conditions with no love or compassion, but the REALLY bad stuff is downstairs! It's there that El accidentally opened the mothergate to the Upside Down while Dr Brenner pushed her to make contact with the Demogorgon. In every way, Hawkins lab is at the very centre of everything that unfolds throughout *Stranger Things*.

HAWKINS MIDDLE SCHOOL

In the first two seasons, the guys are all at Hawkins Middle School. It's the setting for some important parts of the story. The gang use Mr Clarke's Heathkit radio to listen in on Will talking to Joyce from the Upside Down, and it's where they set up their makeshift isolation tank for Eleven to try and find Will. It also provided the backdrop for the Snow Ball, where everyone got to relax for a change!

THE PALACE ARCADE

This is where the guys love to hang out and rival each other's highest score on the latest games (untill Max arrives and shows them all how it's really done!).

The games available include *Dig Dug*, *Pac-Man*, *Asteroids* and *Galaga* – all absolute classics – as well as *Dragon's Lair*, the first Laser Disc game which cost 50 cents to play instead of the usual 25 cents!

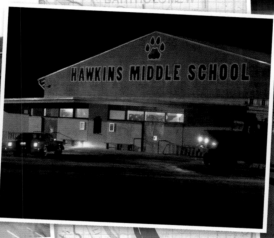

DID YOU SPOT THEM?

CHIEF OF POLICE

Jaws actually came out in theatres in 1975, but it was still hugely popular in the 80s. Martin Brodie, the Chief of Police in *Jaws*, has a lot in common with Jim Hopper, with them both looking after small, scared communities. The similarities don't end there though – check out how similar their badges are!

Stranger Things is LOADED with authentic 80s references and hidden meanings! Here's a look at some of the subtle – and not-so-subtle – references in the series.

ELEVEN PHONE HOME

When the boys try to disguise El by giving her a blonde wig and a pink dress, she looks kinda...familiar. That's because that scene is TOTALLY inspired by a scene from the brilliant *E.T.*, directed by the equally brilliant Steven Spielberg!

PHOENIX RISING

A huge *X-Men* reference is at the very start of Season 1. Will asks for Dustin's *X-Men* #134 comic if he beats him home, just before he goes missing. That issue covers the story of Jean Grey's transition to Dark Phoenix – a character with unstable telekinetic energy. Hmm, who does that sound like? Other links include El's showdown with the Demogorgon mirroring a scene from that comic almost exactly, while Hellfire Club is the name of a group in the *X-Men* universe that tries to control Jean Grey!

CALL ME!

In episode Season 3, we briefly see Murray's phone number – 618-625-8313. Amazingly, it's real! If you call the number in the US, then you'll reach Murray's voicemail message for Joyce. In Season 4, the same thing happens with Surfer Boy Pizza – if you call 805-45-74992 then you get through to a recorded message from Argyle!

STAND BY ME

There's a nod to *Stand By Me*, a film based on a Stephen King book and one that covers the friendship between a group of children (sounds familiar, right?) When Dustin and Steve walk along train tracks in the woods, it's a clear tribute to one of the most famous scenes in *Stand By Me*.

WHO YA GONNA CALL?

Now here's an easter egg that works TWO ways. In Season 2, the boys dress up as the Ghostbusters (albeit with two Venkmans and no Winston). The outfits are spot on in homage to one of the biggest films of the 80s. Here's the kicker though – Finn Wolfhard (who plays Mike) went on to star in *Ghostbusters: Afterlife* four years later!

LOTS OF TOYS

There are loads of references to the toys of the 80s in *Stranger Things*! When Mike is sorting toys to give away, he goes through a treasure trove as he decides! He wisely saves a Millennium Falcon, but he gave away figures of He-Man and Man-At-Arms from Masters of the Universe – they'd be worth over £2,000 between them today. DOH! We also see more Star Wars toys in Season 3, when El controls them and some Transformers to surprise Dustin!

THE MASTER OF HORROR

Stephen King was a huge inspiration for the Duffer brothers and *Stranger Things* is littered with King references. These include Lucas reading a copy of *The Talisman* to Max, while Joyce's scene with the axe is reference to the iconic 'heeeere's Johnny' scene from *The Shining* (which you probably know even if you haven't seen the film).

SHOOTING HOOPS

In Season 4, Lucas' basketball shirt number, 8, is the same number that Kobe Bryant used to wear. Actor Caleb McLaughlin specifically asked for the number, in tribute to one of his heroes.

THE GOONIES

Another film that's all about a group of friends uniting on a mission that most adults believe is just make-believe, *The Goonies* has a very similar feel to *Stranger Things*. Also, one of the child stars of *The Goonies*, Sean Astin, plays Bob Newby!

NIGHTMARE IN HAWKINS

Wes Craven's *Nightmare on Elm Street* is one of the most influential horror movies ever made, so it's no surprise that this 1984 classic has also been given the *Stranger Things* treatment. Lots of viewers noticed that Vecna has more than a passing resemblance to everyone's favourite boogeyman Freddy Krueger. The link goes deeper though – Robert Englund, who played Krueger, stars as Victor Creel!

LEAVE YOUR HAT ON

As well as having a Jaws-themed influence (see page 30) Hopper's rugged look pays tribute to another grizzled good guy who seems unapproachable but has a heart of gold. Step forward Indiana Jones! When actor David Harbour secured the role of Hopper, he insisted that the character wore a wide-brimmed fedora hat so that he would look like the famous fictional archaeologist!

LOGO AGOGO

Stephen King probably had more influence on *Stranger Things* than anyone else on this list – but his impact went beyond storylines and subtle references. The name *Stranger Things* was chosen as it was very similar to one of King's books, *Needful Things*, and the logo pays homage to the fonts used on the covers of King's books. Little wonder, then, that the *Stranger Things* logo is so instantly recognisable and conjures up that retro feel with ease - just look how alike they are!

SEASON 3 BEST BITS

Some great new characters joined the cast for Season 3, along with a terrifying new threat to Hawkins' very existence. Eek!

BAD BOY GETS...BADDER!

Ok, so Billy is hardly the nicest guy in Hawkins, but even he doesn't deserve what happens to him at the start of Season 3. Poor guy thinks he's off for a hot date with Karen Wheeler, but something smashes his car off the road while he's practicing his chat-up lines. The segment where he is confronted by himself is spinechilling.

TEAM BATTLE!

Talk about David Vs Goliath! As the mind flayed Tom and Bruce chase Nancy and Jonathan through the corridors of Hawkins Memorial Hospital, it feels like there can only be one winner. However, brains always beats brawn and Nancy gets the edge by hiding then surprising Bruce with a fire extinguisher to the face! Watching Tom and Bruce feel each others pain is satisfying, as is watching them melt away into mush after they've been beaten!

RESPECT MY AUTHORITY

The second Hopper shuts Mayor Kline's door, you just know something bad is going to go down. And Hopper doesn't take Larry's pathetic attempts to deny all knowledge of who attacked him very well at all. That said, while everyone knew Hopper was mad enough to get physical, it was hard not to look away when he was considering a new use for poor Larry's cigar cutter, wasn't it?

WHAT'S IN IT FOR ERICA?

For the first two seasons, Erica was just a bit of comic relief as Lucas' little sister. She soon graduates with honours though, when the team realises that she is the only person who can fit in the vents at Starcourt Mall, meaning she's the only one who can find out what's really happening beneath the mall. What's more, she shows she may be small, but she is FIERCE by carrying out the task – and insisting on eating her own bodyweight in ice cream!

SHOP 'TIL YOU DROP

Life in a scientific research lab means a person misses out on some pretty key experiences – so it's super cute when Max and Eleven bond by undertaking the girliest of shopping sprees! The outfits are all eighties-tastic, and in a pretty intense storyline, you can't help but smile at two girls just having fun, can you?

WELCOME HOME!

After a long summer at Science Camp, Dustin is just settling back home when his toys start moving of their own accord, leading him into the lounge. That's when we see the toys are under El's command, as the gang leap out to surprise him. It doesn't end well, with a panicked Dustin spraying Farrah Fawcett hairspray into Lucas' face!

CLEVER JOYCE

It must drive Joyce mad that no-one listens to her first time – especially when she's usually right! Her fridge magnet obsession is dismissed by Hopper, but on a visit to Mr Clarke's garage, his impromptu experiment gives her food for thought that would ultimately lead her to Hawkins lab as the bad guys once again...

BROMANCE ALERT!

The unlikely besties that are Dustin and Steve melt hearts every time they are on-screen together but even they out-cuted themselves with their special handshake in Scoops Ahoy! It's made even funnier by being watched by an exasperated Robin, who doesn't even try to hide her contempt!

BILLY SAVES ELEVEN

As the battle for Starcourt Mall rages, it looks like poor El is a gonner, as Billy – under the control of the Mind Flayer – drags her, barely conscious, so she can be sacrificed. But when El connects with the REAL Billy, deep down inside, he's able to channel the last of his humanity to throw himself in the way, saving Eleven in the process. Billy dies a hero. Who'd have thought it, huh?

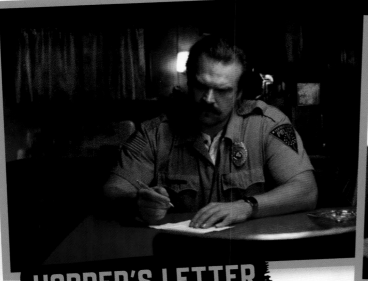

HOPPER'S LETTER

The closing scene, as Hopper's letter is read out from beyond the grave, is unforgettable. His love for Eleven, and how she taught him to open his heart again, means there's not a dry eye in the house. Guaranteed to get you in the feels every single time.

TURN TO **PAGE 48** FOR
SEASON 4 BEST BITS

NANCY WHEELER

Never judge a book by its cover! Nancy Wheeler is definitely NOT someone to mess with!

When we first meet nancy, it seems all she's interested in is boys and parties and looking 'cool'. When her best friend Barb suddenly disappears, all that changes and Nancy gets serious pretty much overnight. She is on the hunt for the truth and refuses to give up no matter what. She might look like a standard highschooler, but Nancy is a woman who will dive head first in to the Upside Down time and time again to save her friends, and has faced the Demogorgon, Mind Flayer and Vecna, and won! Nancy is Definitely NOT someone to mess with!

I WANT TO FINISH WHAT I STARTED. I WANT TO KILL IT.

NANCY DREW

Nancy is super smart as well as being brave and resourceful. She's a great student (even though she does kinda goof off a bit once she gets with Steve) and is the driving force behind the Hawkins High school newspaper too. She's often the first in the group to spot new leads and solves problems (like working out that Max's scribbles revealed Vecna's hiding place).

"HEY, WANNA DANCE?"

Between the epic moments of bravery, Nancy will also show her softer side from time-to-time when it comes to her friends. When she see's Dustin getting rejected at the Snow Ball dance by a group of girls, she takes his hand and dances with him in view of everyone, making Dustin feel like a king while the girls look on awkwardly. Nancy Wheeler, you're a big softie really!

MEET

JONATHAN BYERS

Big brother Jonathan is a quiet, introverted kind of guy. That often means he's misunderstood by those around him.

Without really getting to know Jonathan, many people think he's weird just for liking his own company – even though there's nothing wrong with that! In fact, Jonathan is an inquisitive guy who explores the world around him through his camera lens, which is actually what leads Nancy to the realisation that there is more to Barb's disappearance than first thought! His loyalty and bravery mean he plays a key part in rescuing Will and then keeping the town safe – that's how good big brothers roll.

MORE THAN GOOD FRIENDS...

Jonathan's relationship with Nancy is the definition of a slow burn! She's with the 'cooler' Steve to start with, but quickly finds that she has much more in common with Jonathan's intellect and artistic streak. Seeing them develop as a couple is one of the highlights of the first half of *Stranger Things*!

> " NOBODY NORMAL EVER ACCOMPLISHED ANYTHING MEANINGFUL IN THIS WORLD "

BROTHERS IN ARMS

Jonathan is a fiercely protective big brother, but he and Will grow apart a little as they get older. But Jonathan always has his brother's back and the heart-to-heart they have in the pizza kitchen means so much to Will – to know his big brother loves him, and always will, no matter what. We're not crying, you're crying.

MEET

STEVE HARRINGTON

Life is all about journeys and finding out who you truly are, and Steve certainly goes on quite a transformation!

To start with, he is the classic high school Mr Popular! He chases girls, and doesn't care about anything other than partying and having fun. Talk about rising to the challenge though – he shows us he has way more depth than that as the seasons unfold, becoming a great friend and ally to the gang whatever the Upside Down throws at them. Fearless Harrington faces everything that comes his way, whether it's a rampaging Billy, or a brutal interrogation from the Russian military, Steve gets up, runs his fingers through his hair and is ready for whatever comes his way!

> **WOULD YOU GUYS LIKE TO SET SAIL ON THIS OCEAN OF FLAVOR WITH ME?**

"I GOT A JOB!"

Steve has had more jobs than he can probably remember! In the short time that *Stranger Things* is set, he has worked in the local movie theatre, as a babysitter, in Scoops Ahoy, the ice cream parlour in Starcourt Mall and finally (for now!) in the Hawkins branch of Family Video!

A TURNING POINT

One of the moments that starts Steve's transformation is his fight with Jonathan. When Steve taunted Jonathan in to a physical confrontation after dissing the Byers name, and came out worse, it made him think about the kind of guy he was becoming, and he changed his path – thankfully!

40

ROBIN BUCKLEY

Seems weird to think that we didn't even meet Robin until Season 3 working at Scoops Ahoy in Starcourt Mall.

Her friendship with Steve as they work dead end jobs together with a beautiful mixture of cynicism and humour is one of the best bits of Seasons 3 and 4. Robin is also one of the smartest people ever to serve ice cream – she's fluent in four languages and it's her ability to translate Russian that ultimately helps unravel the mysterious message and reveals the plot in Season 3!

LOVE IS LOVE

One of the most beautifully written parts of *Stranger Things* is when Robin comes out as gay to Steve in a mall bathroom.. After Steve admits that he's crazy about Robin, she responds by telling him her high school crush was on Tammy Thompson – a girl in their English class. Steve's relaxed response to his friend coming out is exactly as it should be – friendly and accepting.

> " **YOU THINK YOU'RE SO SMART, BUT A COUPLE OF KIDS WHO SCOOP ICE CREAM FOR A LIVING CRACKED YOUR CODE IN A DAY** "

YOU SUCK!

As well as being bright, Robin is super sarcastic and loves nothing more than teasing poor Steve. When he hits on customers at Scoops Ahoy, she keeps a score of his efforts on a 'You Rule/You Suck' chart and she also loves to mess with customers she doesn't like (especially any that abuse the free sample policy at Scoops Ahoy!)

STRIKE A POSE

The 80s was an amazing decade for fashion – and some of the things people wore back then are making a comeback (partly thanks to series like *Stranger Things*). Here's a look at some of the 80s trends you might want to work into your own wardrobe.

BRACES

Don't worry, we're not talking about what you get at the dentist. In the 80s, if you said you were wearing braces, it would mean the elasticated bands that hook over your shoulders from the waistband of your jeans. El wears brightly coloured braces twice in the series, and it's a cool look. Practical too, if your trousers are a bit on the big side!

BIG HAIR

Bouffant hair was all the rage in the 80s, and not just on the girls! The air was thick with the smell of hairspray with the theme very often being 'the bigger the better'! Just ask Dustin and Nancy.

BRIGHT COLOURS

Standing out in the 80s must have been impossible because everyone wore such bright colours. There are lots of colourful outfits in *Stranger Things*, mainly worn for special events or when the characters are 'dressing up'. Bright colours were often matched with crazy patterns too. It's enough to give anyone a headache!

JUMPSUITS

Now here's a trend that is bang up-to-date. In fact, El's legendary jumpsuit was the focus of much online debate with people certain it was a recent design, but the wardrobe department confirmed it was an 80s original. Definitely an easy item to rock in the 2020s, but one that very much has its roots in the 80s.

SCOOPS AHOY

The uniforms that Steve and Robin wear when working in Scoops Ahoy would make any right-minded individual want to hide (including them) but for reasons no-one knows, silly outfits were surprisingly common for 80s restaurants. Stripes, hats, outfits, silly colours – you name it, in the 1980s you were probably served food by someone wearing it.

FLOWERY SHIRTS

Flower power didn't die out in the 70s you know! It was alive and well in the 80s, with men's casual shirts being all the rage. Popular shows like *Hawaii 5-0* and *Magnum PI* helped shops shift even more brightly coloured shirts – Hopper is definitely a fan and is even seen watching *Magnum* in Season 1 before dressing like him on a date!

DENIM

Denim was THE default look for anyone into rock music. Fashion has a love/hate relationship with denim, especially denim jackets, but the success of *Stranger Things* has definitely helped even double denim (jeans paired with a denim jacket) to be cool again!

THE 80s
TOP TECH

The 1980s were an innovative time, and lots of the gadgets we take for granted now have developed from things around at the time. Today, however, some of the tech looks pretty prehistoric – and you might not even know what some of it is, or how it works! Here's a look at some of the gadgets that feature in *Stranger Things*!

WALKMANS

These were all the rage in the 80s – a tiny cassette player and a set of headphones so you could listen to music on the go! You can see them used often, most memorably as the gang battle to save Max by finding her favourite song!

THESE DAYS: You just listen to music on an app!

VHS

VHS tapes were the only way to watch the latest movies at home in the 80s. Most people rented them from video stores, and Steve and Robin's employer, Family Video was a real chain in the USA! VHS quality was not great, and they got worse the more they were watched!

THESE DAYS: Well, how did you watch *Stranger Things* in the first place? Through Netflix of course, one of many streaming services that deliver movies and TV series straight to your TV (or phone!) whenever you want it. Sooooo much easier!

CRT TELEVISIONS

TVs in the 80s were big. No, we don't mean popular, we mean MASSIVE. Lots didn't even have remote controls either – you had to get up to change the channel! In Season 2, El used her powers to stop Hopper from lifting the TV when they had an argument, he probably wasn't even acting as he struggled to pick it up!

THESE DAYS: All TVs are now less than two inches thick, with amazing picture quality and are as light as a feather. To wall mount an 80s television you'd have needed a seriously strong shelf and a degree in engineering.

CAMCORDERS

Recording your own footage was a mission in the 80s. Camcorders recorded onto tape and there was pretty much nothing you could do to edit your films. The sound and vision quality of even the good camcorders was dreadful by modern standards!

THESE DAYS: You can record crystal-clear footage on a smartphone or mobile device, and there are thousands of brilliant editing apps available to make your masterpiece!

DEC 15.84   7:04 PM

STEREOS

Like TVs, the size of a stereo in the 80s was huge. Just look at the set Will plays music through in Season 1. They'd usually feature a record player and two tape decks along with two huge speakers to listen to music through. The technology required to make it all possible meant that the device was gigantic!

THESE DAYS: You can get the same effect from tiny wireless speakers or sound bars that can even mimic things like surround sound. Insane.

TALK TO FRIENDS

In the 80s, this involved walkie talkies or radio broadcasts. Your mate would need to be tuned into the right frequency and all kinds of things could mess up the signal (trees, pylons, passing lorries, you name it...) It wasn't easy to have a conversation lasting more than a few minutes – and those things ATE batteries for fun!

THESE DAYS: Life couldn't be easier! You send a voice note, or a text message, or make a call, from your mobile phone. The very idea of a tiny phone you could carry in your pocket would have been about as believable in 1980 as Demogorgons running riot in Indiana!

WORDSEARCH

Can you find the following words from *Stranger Things* in our wordsearch?

- UPSIDE DOWN
- HAWKINS
- DEMOGORGON
- BYERS
- HOPPER
- ELEVEN
- EGGOS
- DUSTIN
- MIND FLAYER
- VECNA
- PALACE
- LUCAS
- SCOOPS AHOY
- INDIANA
- BRENNER
- TELEKENISIS
- ARCADE

D	P	T	C	P	N	Y	U	W	L	V	I	O	A	H
X	U	E	P	A	L	A	C	E	E	I	J	N	A	M
S	D	S	H	B	D	R	O	C	J	T	A	W	J	I
R	W	D	T	L	X	W	N	F	K	I	K	Y	S	N
U	W	N	S	I	L	A	T	X	D	I	C	O	H	D
P	R	S	C	R	N	I	R	N	N	T	I	H	O	F
S	H	J	A	E	E	N	I	S	J	X	U	A	P	L
I	G	G	R	C	E	Y	E	G	G	O	S	S	P	A
D	F	E	T	V	U	K	B	M	E	M	N	P	E	Y
E	F	B	E	F	H	L	J	X	D	D	S	O	R	E
D	X	L	B	R	E	N	N	E	R	D	A	O	N	R
O	E	H	U	K	K	S	V	P	A	I	J	C	U	U
W	N	O	G	R	O	G	O	M	E	D	W	S	R	F
N	O	T	E	L	E	K	E	N	I	S	I	S	N	A
L	P	P	J	A	C	B	M	D	F	F	O	Q	M	M

Remember that words can run up, down, across and diagonally and in any direction!

LEAVING
HAWKINS
COME AGAIN SOON

Original - Originale

Kellogg's Eggo

46

CROSSWORD

ANSWERS ON PAGE 78

ACROSS

3 _____ & Dragons, the name of the fantasy game the boys love so much (8)

8 The name of the arcade hall in Hawkins where the gang hangs out (3,6)

9 Where poor Barb meets her end in Season 1 (8,4)

12 The guitar epic that Eddie Munson plays to lure the Demobats (6,2,7)

14 The name given to the alternate dimension where Will is taken (6,4)

15 The first message Will sends to Joyce through the Christmas lights (5,4)

17 The full name of the baby Demodog that Dustin finds and adopts at the start of Season 2 (9)

DOWN

1 The monster the gang must defeat in Season 4 (5)

2 Lucas' surname (8)

4 The name of the actor who played Will Byers (4,7)

5 The name of the D&D club at Hawkins High (8,4)

6 Jim Hopper's job in Hawkins (5,2,6)

7 Eleven's favourite snack (5)

10 The name of the girl with ESP powers (6)

11 The state the Byers move to in Season 4 (10)

13 The state that is home to Hawkins (7)

16 The name of Billy's younger sister (3)

SEASON 4
BEST BITS

At the end of every season you think *Stranger Things* can't get better – and every season it does! How do the Duffer Brothers do it? Here are some of the high points of Season 4!

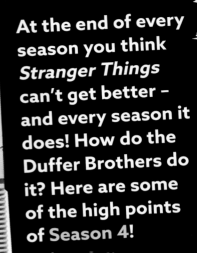

D&D MEETS BASKETBALL

The Duffer brothers are absolute masters of telling two stories at the same time that mirror each other, and this is probably the best example in the whole series.

As Lucas battles to help Hawkins High win their basketball semi-final, his sister Erika has taken his place in Hellfire Club. Lucas' battle between becoming a 'cool kid' and staying true to his friends is brilliantly handled, showing the dilemma the poor guy is in at every turn.

VECNA'S FIRST VICTIM

Poor old Eddie. A girl he really fancies opens up to him, and even comes round to his place – only for Vecna to put her into a trance and become his first victim. The absolute horror of her final moments terrifies poor Eddie – who knows that no-one will believe his story of levitation and bones seeming to snap on their own.

BREAKING FREE

Once we'd all stopped high-fiving each other at the news that Hopper was still alive, attention turned to how he would get out of that Russian prison camp. Of course Hop came through, with a plot involving a bit of bribery, a broken sledgehammer, an exploding tool shed and escaping on a snowmobile amid a hail of Russian bullets. Standard day at the office.

RUNNING UP THAT HILL

One of THE scenes that you'll remember for the rest of your life. The horror of Vecna's attempts to kill Max while the boys scrabble to play her favourite song through her Walkman is absolute edge-of-the-seat stuff. Her levitation as she battles her way back despite Vecna's best efforts is phenomenal and it's a scene you could watch on a loop and never get bored with.

THE KARATE KID

Murray's such a funny character and often provides a bit of comedy in otherwise dark scenes. Although Murray admits to going to karate classes every Tuesday, he has always made out he is absolutely useless at it and would lose in a fight with a child. Until it's showtime against Yuri and POW! The man's Jackie Chan, Chuck Norris and Bruce Lee rolled into one!

THE FACE OF EVIL

The slow coming together of Vecna's back story is brilliantly handled in *Stranger Things*. The sequence pulls together loads of little threads perfectly so you feel like you've figured out the whole One/Henry Creel/Vecna thing by yourself rather than just having it thrown at you.
It's expertly done!

OFF WITH YOUR HEAD

After an epic sequence, Hopper empties a shotgun at the Demogorgon but barely scratches it. Grabbing a sword from the floor, he makes a desperate swing, taking the Demogorgon's arm off. Hoppers next attack is even better – he removes its head!

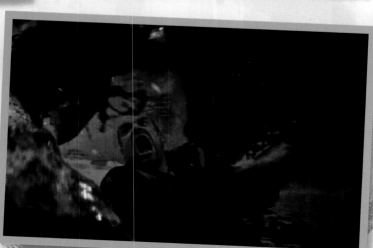

THE FINAL STAND

When Steve, Robin and Nancy find Vecna hanging from his vines in a trance-like state, they knew this was the best chance to end him. The gang grab their Molotov cocktails and rain FIRE on Vecna! Followed up with a few shotgun blasts later from Nancy, knocking Vecna out of the attic window, it's game over for the bad guy...or is it?

HE WAS A HERO

As Eddie's grief-stricken uncle puts up posters asking people to look for his nephew, Dustin takes the opportunity to sit with him and tell him about Eddie's heroic death, and how much Eddie was loved. It's a real tear-jerker but a beautiful scene. We just wish that the people of Hawkins had got to know the real Eddie!

THE FINAL GATES OPEN

Just when it looks like Vecna has killed Max, Eleven manages to bring her back – but not before the gates merged, as Vecna gained enough power to do so while Max was 'dead'. The result is devastating destruction to the town of Hawkins, and we leave the gang looking down on the burning ruins of their home town knowing that another epic battle lies ahead of them.

MEET

MAX MAYFIELD

Max joins the gang in Season 2 after she moves from California to Hawkins with her mum, stepdad and stepbrother Billy.

To start with, she's not at all bothered about befriending Will, Mike, Lucas and Dustin, but they do eventually make friends and she becomes part of the gang after they all meet up during a night of trick-or-treating. Max's difficult family life means that she is very independent, and is not afraid to disagree with the boys and stand up to them when she thinks they are wrong (quite right too!) But we soon see that Max is willing to stand up to more than just the boys when it comes to saving her friends and her new home, Hawkins.

THERE'S MORE TO LIFE THAN STUPID BOYS, YOU KNOW.

SKATER GIRL

One of the coolest things about Max is how she does things the boys love WAY better than they can. She's a very gifted skater but even better than that, she doesn't show off to impress – she just does her thing. And of course when the boys realise that the new girl at school is MADMAX from the arcade that has smashed all the top scores, the boys are super jealous!

GIRL POWER

Max is a really crucial part of the gang, especially for Eleven. Having spent her whole life in an institution and then hanging out with boys, Eleven lacks a gal pal – a role that Max takes on with style! Makeovers, boy talk, girly shopping trips, you name it and those besties do it!

MEET

BILLY HARGROVE

Billy (or should that be 'Bully'?) is Max's older stepbrother and is not a nice guy however you look at it.

He's aggressive and downright violent towards Max and her mum, and he also throws his weight around with Steve and Lucas. But you never know what someone's going through, right? Turns out that Billy had a pretty messed up childhood, which explains a lot. Deep down, he isn't all bad, as he shows by making the ultimate sacrifice to save the sister he loves (even if he's not good at showing it).

LIKE A HURRICANE

How a character makes an entrance can be crucial. Billy's approach is perfect – cruising up to school in his Camara with 'Rock You Like a Hurricane' by the Scorpions blasting out of the stereo at full volume. Sums his rebel bad boy persona up pretty much perfectly, wouldn't you say?

" AND YOU KNOW WHAT HAPPENS WHEN YOU DISOBEY ME. I BREAK THINGS. "

LET'S GET READY TO RUMBLE

Billy and Steve are two of the most volatile characters in *Stranger Things*, all tight jeans, big hair and testosterone. No surprise that they end up getting fisty with each other at the end of Season 2. The scene is absolutely intense – it'll take your breath away and leave you needing a bit of quiet time!

EDDIE MUNSON

Look up 'cool' in the dictionary, and there'll be a picture of Eddie Munson. Ok, there won't be. But there should be.

Eddie is a rare creature – he does the cool stuff like playing in a rock band, and loves the geeky stuff like being Dungeon Master for the D&D adventures of the Hellfire Club. He's a man who knows who he is, basically, and doesn't pretend to be anything he's not. He's loyal, kind and charismatic, but his rugged rock star appearance can give the wrong first impression until you get to know him - never judge a book by it's cover! Eddie is responsible for THAT epic scene set to 'Master of Puppets'. He's an absolute Hawkins legend to those who got to know the real Eddie.

> " **I THINK IT'S MY YEAR, HENDERSON. I THINK IT'S FINALLY MY YEAR!** "

A HEART OF GOLD

One of Eddie's best features is how he is happy to include people. He bases his decisions purely on whether he likes someone or not. That's how he ends up welcoming Lucas' sister, Erica, to the Hellfire Club (after initially not being sure). And it's how he comes to give such confidence and acceptance to our wonderful band of dweebs, geeks and misfits – all while being the coolest guy around!

HE DIDN'T RUN AWAY

There's no way we can mention Eddie without talking about his dramatic end scene. By shredding 'Master of Puppets' on his guitar, Eddie keeps the Demobats' attention on him and gives his friends the chance they need. So sad that his injuries were too much for him to survive.

MEET

DR BRENNER

If *Stranger Things* was a pantomime, Dr Brenner is the dude we'd all be booing.

He positively reeks of evil and seems to have no morals at all. Taking kids from their family? Check. Implanting chips in children's brains? Check. Trying to harness evil forces from another dimension for his own evil purposes? Check!! And he's like a cockroach – it looked like he was a goner at the end of Season 1, but oh no – back he crawls in Season 4. At least he FINALLY gets what he deserves at the very end.

POWER HUNGRY!

Nothing sums Brenner up better than his fascination with the Demogorgon. Any normal person would have run a mile, but Brenner's thirst for power means he tries to harness the power of the Demogorgon – and of course it ends up killing his whole crew and very nearly killing Brenner himself.

> ## ONLY BY FACING ALL OF OURSELVES, THE GOOD AND THE BAD, CAN WE BECOME WHOLE.

TOO LATE FOR 'SORRY'

The thing with people like Brenner is they ALWAYS think that deep down they are good people. Even right at the end, as he lies dying in the sand, he tells Eleven that he loves her and only ever wanted to help her (funny way to show it, pal). Her simple response of 'Goodbye, Papa' shows that she doesn't forgive him. And nor should she!

DR OWENS

Dr Owens (Samuel to his friends) is proof that you can work for a top-secret government agency tasked with suppressing the truth and still be a good guy. After taking over from Dr Brenner, he shows far more kindness and compassion while doing his job. He makes a good point too – if a weapon like the Upside Down fell into the wrong hands, it would be far worse!

MURRAY BAUMAN

Murray is an absolute legend. Hired as a private eye to figure out what happened to Barb (about time somebody cared!), he figures out that there's definitely Russian involvement and eventually the team bring him on board to work together. It was Murray who figured out there was much more to Joyce's delivery than a Russian doll and you can tell he's a good detective as he figured out that Joyce and Hopper should get it together after making the same observation to Nancy and Jonathan!

DMITRI ANTONOV

Dmitri is the man who gets the ball rolling in Season 4, accepting a bribe from Hopper to send Joyce the doll that tells her he is ALIVE! After helping Hopper plot a route to escape, they're both double-crossed and poor Dmitri ends up inside the prison he once guarded! Dmitri is a brave and sensitive guy, bonding with Hopper when they are both inmates, and showing courage as they escape from the Demogorgon in the battle at the prison camp.

ARGYLE

Surfs up dudes! Argyle is the gnarly and downright BODACIOUS delivery boy for Surfer Boy Pizza. He has a heart of gold (and possibly a brain of wool) and befriends Jonathan, giving him love-life advice. When the soldiers attack the Byers, Argyle rescues them, propelling himself into the adventures. He reacts like any chilled-out dude would – just takes everything in his stride and keeps the sunshine coming. It's still a no to pineapple on pizza though, Argyle, no matter how nice you are.

SUZIE BINGHAM

Suzie is proof that sometimes, the good guy does get the girl! She brings an end to Dustin's run of being unlucky in love when they meet at Camp Know Where, and stay in touch via long range radio. Their shared geeky streak is there for all to see, though she does have embarrassing girlfriend potential. All together now: 'The never-ending stoooorrryyyyyy....'

JASON CARVER

As a good-looking all-American sports jock, Jason was never going to get on well with our beloved gang. His obsession with blaming Eddie for Chrissy's death, and his determination for revenge, was all about his own anger, not justice for Chrissy. Ultimately, it is what leads to his doom. Can't say he'll be missed too much...

SEASON 3&4
WHERE IT HAPPENED

HAWKINS COMMUNITY POOL

Ah, nothing shouts fun like a pool party, does it? This community facility is full of kids having fun, teenagers misbehaving and mums meeting to gossip and watch the world go by. It's where Billy works but proves a less happy place when he is given a free sauna session against his will!

BRIMBORN STEEL WORKS

An abandoned warehouse on the outskirts of town, shrouded in darkness. What could possibly go wrong? It certainly made the perfect venue for the Mind Flayer. With no-one snooping around, the Mind Flayer was able to attract rats and then humans to use in its quest for a physical form.

STARCOURT MALL

A lively shopping mall full of milkshakes and ice cream parlours to the big stores of the day. Sadly, this idyllic retail heaven hides a dark secret – namely the portal to a hellish alternate dimension that the Russian Army has opened in the basement. The battle of Starcourt Mall is perhaps the most iconic sequence in the whole series so far.

KAMCHATKA PRISON CAMP

The snow-blasted prison camp that Hopper is sent to in Russia, Kamchatka doesn't need Demogorgons or other-worldly activity to be scary – it's already downright scary! The buildings are ramshackle and badly maintained, and the whole place screams of menace and misery. No wonder Hopper was so desperate to escape.

THE NINA PROJECT

It might just look like a tiny hut in the middle of the Nevada Desert when Eleven is taken there by Dr Owens, but the true horror of the Nina Project is all underground. It's a very sophisticated sensory deprivation tank which Dr Brenner believes will help Eleven to recover the powers that she lost after closing the gate at the end of Season 3. It doesn't end well.

THE CREEL HOUSE

The backstory of Vecna's creation is a truly terrifying one, and all the scarier for being set in a seemingly normal residence. Knowing the backstory of how Vecna came to be, it makes sense that the hellish creature would return here to connect to his tendrils of evil.

DUNGEONS & DRAGONS EXPLAINED

At the heart of the friendship between the gang is the Hellfire Club, and the Dungeons & Dragons adventures that the boys enjoy together. But what IS Dungeons & Dragons, and how can you get involved for yourself?

Dungeons & Dragons (or D&D for short) is a fantasy role-playing game that is played in a small group, with one player acting as the storyteller (the 'Dungeon Master' or DM) and the other players controlling a character each and working together to complete quests in a fantasy world.

The fantastic thing about D&D is that it doesn't require a 4K television or expensive figurines and a tabletop battlefield. The adventures unwind in the minds of the players, driven by the DM who tells the story and conjures up the sights, sounds and smells that surround the players as their quest unfolds.

ADVANCED DUNGEONS & DRAGONS DUNGEON MASTER'S SCREEN

You can create your own character – sometimes it will be a completely new one, but players often keep their character and take them on newer, more complex quests as they grow and develop. You'll choose a race (such as human, dwarf, elf etc) and a class (wizard, fighter, medic etc).

HELLFIRE CLUB

The DM will describe what is happening as the action unfolds, setting up events where the outcome is decided by the roll of a dice. This includes combat, with players taking it in turns to roll a dice and see if they are able to damage their opponent until there is a winner and a loser. The DM will roll the dice for the non-player characters (NPCs), but they are not 'against' the rest of the party – they are there more as a guide and a referee, part player, part storyteller.

More experienced DMs will make up entire campaigns in their head, relying on their knowledge of the game alone. However, there are also lots of campaign guides for less experienced DMs, providing help and inspiration for anyone looking to get into the series. You can pick up a D&D starter kit for around £20 from the usual online retailers – an absolute bargain! Why not club together with a few friends and start your own Hellfire Club?

MONSTER

DEMOGORGON

This large, humanoid monster has long, gangly limbs and a flower-like head. However, when the flower 'opens' there's nothing pleasant inside — just sharp teeth that are hungry for human flesh! The Demogorgon is a fearsome hunter, tracking prey down with heightened smell and hearing.

SIZE: 2.75M　**POWER: 7**
FEAR FACTOR: 9

DEMODOG

Demodogs, as the name suggests, are fearsome hunters who work as a pack. They are incredibly nimble, able to climb walls and squeeze through tiny gaps in pursuit of their prey. They're also very intelligent, with fearsome teeth and jaws — just ask poor Bob Newby!

SIZE: 1.2M　**POWER: 6**
FEAR FACTOR: 8

DEMOBAT

They may be small, but the real fear factor with demobats is the sheer scale of the numbers they can attack in. They attack as a colony, and no matter how many you can take out, they'll just keep coming. Their excellent hearing helps make them even harder to avoid, as they'll zero in on their prey at the slightest sound.

SIZE: 0.5M　**POWER: 4**
FEAR FACTOR: 7

SPIDER MONSTER

The Spider Monster is a horrifying creature created by the Mind Flayer from the remains of the humans and animals that it has previously controlled. With sharp teeth and incredible strength, it's also absolutely huge — filling the centre of Starcourt Mall!

SIZE: 9.2M　**POWER: 8**
FEAR FACTOR: 10

MADNESS

COME OUT FROM BEHIND THAT SOFA AND TAKE A LOOK AT SOME OF THE MONSTERS THAT HAVE GIVEN US (AND THE RESIDENTS OF HAWKINS) SLEEPLESS NIGHTS!

THE MIND FLAYER

The Mind Flayer is an ethereal creature from the Upside Down that was able to escape after creating a bond with Henry Creel. Its initial form is a storm-like collection of particles, but it has the ability to control the minds of humans and animals, as well as create monsters of its own.

SIZE: 18.3M **POWER: 9**
FEAR FACTOR: 10

DR BRENNER

He may not be a monster in the traditional sense of the word, but Brenner's complete lack of morals and his willingness to experiment on young children make him perhaps the scariest monster in Hawkins. A man who will do anything for power, he's definitely someone to avoid.

SIZE: 1.85M **POWER: 2**
FEAR FACTOR: 6

THE FLAYED

An unfortunate mob of zombie-like people, The Flayed are people (and animals) who are unfortunate enough to have their minds taken over by the Mind Flayer. Forced to carry out evil, the Mind Flayer uses them as an expendable, seemingly never-ending army to attack its enemies.

SIZE: 1.75M **POWER: 5**
FEAR FACTOR: 8

VECNA

Formerly Number One (and Henry Creel before that) Vecna is a powerful sorcerer full of rage and hate. When Creel was banished to The Upside Down by Eleven, he became Vecna over time — and his determination to seek revenge on a world that hated him is what drives him on.

SIZE: 1.85M **POWER: 10**
FEAR FACTOR: 10

THE THREE FACES OF TERROR

VECNA

Join us (peeping through your fingers) as we take you through the stages of evil that created Vecna – the most scariest, evil nemesis that any world has ever see, never mind just this one!

THE CHILD

Even Vecna was cute once. Henry Creel was a little boy when he moved to Hawkins with his parents and his big sister. Unfortunately, Henry had dark powers, and didn't really understand that he was even using them, let alone how to use them. Over time, he became able to make the rest of his family hallucinate – cribs on fire, spiders flowing out of the bath taps, all the usual things that would make you lose your mind.

The family thought it was a demon possessing the house. It wasn't. Sadly, Henry was a mean and nasty kid, and when he did realise how to use his powers, he killed his mum and his sister before collapsing into a coma. Of course, his dad Victor got the blame and went to prison for it – but news of Henry's powers reached a certain Dr Brenner who took Henry into his 'care' in Hawkins National Laboratory.

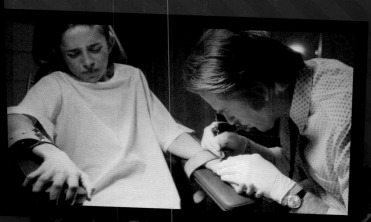

THE EXPERIMENT

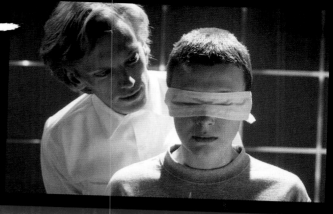

Poor Henry was officially One – the first child in Dr Brenner's nursery of doom. Brenner wanted to replicate those powers in others, so used One as a benchmark for his other experiments – and he had plenty of success. However, Brenner feared One's powers and implanted a chip in his neck designed to stop him from being able to use them. However, One tricked El into removing it before going on a murderous rampage and killing most of the other children.

Misery loves company as they say, and One tried to lure El to the dark side too (anyone else getting *Star Wars* vibes here?). She refused though, and in an epic battle of two gifted minds, she pushed One through a portal to a parallel dimension, ridding this world of his evil. Problem solved, right?

THE DEMON

Wrong! Creel/One's anger and hate were left to manifest in the parallel world, transforming him over time into Vecna, the scariest thing in ANY dimension! Because one hellish scary creature is never enough, Vecna also created the Mind Flayer to allow him to head through into other dimensions. Vecna's thirst for pain and torture, and the sheer pleasure he takes from the suffering he causes, makes him officially the scariest thing on Netflix. Don't have nightmares!

HAWKINS FM

The music in *Stranger Things* sets the tone perfectly to transport us all to the 1980s – and it's full of absolute bangers! There are loads of epic tunes, but some of them stand out just a little bit more due to the way they perfectly accompany a scene.

Here's our top ten but let's face it – the *Stranger Things* soundtrack is all killer, no filler. Your own top ten might look completely different – why don't you fill it in and see?

#10 Pass The Dutchie

1982

Artist: Musical Youth   Features in: Season 4

The first reggae track to feature in *Stranger Things*, 'Pass The Dutchie' is a favourite of Argyle's. He often has it playing in his van as he drives round town – though helping the Byers flee from an armed gunman while it played on the van stereo probably didn't provide the relaxation he was looking for!

#9

If you scan the QR code next to each song, you can listen along yourself on Spotify!

Detroit Rock City

1976

Artist: Kiss   Features in: Season 4

This song brings together the mirror scenes of Lucas' basketball success and his friends defeating Vecna in the Hellfire Club without him. It fades in and out, sometimes loud over the action, and sometimes fading into the background – it's a brilliant choice and a superbly edited section.

#8 HEROES

low noise

Artist: Peter Gabriel   Features in: Season 1

This beautiful cover of a David Bowie original is actually an anachronism – it wasn't recorded until 2010. However, as Will's body is found in the lake, it provides a haunting and beautiful backdrop to a truly emotional scene.

#7

Time After Time
1984

Artist: Cyndi Lauper   Features in: Season 2

This song will always have a special place in Dustin's heart. As it starts playing at the Snow Ball, he strides off confidently to try his luck – but gets nowhere as usual. Seeing him looking dejected, Nancy takes charge, and steps in to dance with Dustin to show she cares about his friendship.

#6 Never Ending Story

1984

Artist: Limahl   Features in: Season 3

Poor, poor Dustin. Most guys have a special song with their loved one, but not all of them are forced into singing it in front of their best friends. Dustin goes with it so that Suzie will help them crack the code – that boy has some pipes!

#5

SHOULD I STAY OR SHOULD I GO?

MS 400

cassette

1982

Artist: The Clash   Features in: Season 1 & 2

This is more than a song – it's a message for Jonathan that will always make him think of his little brother Will. It's frequently heard in the background in Season 1 and also appears in Season 2. It's special to the brothers as Jonathan has happy memories of introducing Will to it at home.

#4

MATERIAL GIRL

1984

Artist: Madonna   Features in: Season 2

This 80s classic soundtracks the shopping trip of a lifetime as El and Max run wild in Starcourt Mall. Crazy outfits, a fashion photoshoot and two friends having fun. The mood of the song perfectly suits the scene.

#3

EVERY BREATH YOU TAKE

1983

Artist: The Police   Features in: Season 2

After the adrenaline and action the gang have been through in Season 2, the Snow Ball gives them the chance to let their hair down and have some fun. The song is the perfect accompaniment as first Lucas and Max and then El and Mike have a smooch on the dance floor.

#2

MASTER OF PUPPETS

1986

Artist: Metallica   Features in: Season 4

It's a song that's all about noise and SHREDDING that guitar, which is why it was the absolute PERFECT choice for Eddie Munson to play in Season 4 to attract the Demobats. It sure gets the heart racing, doesn't it?

#1

Running Up That Hill

1984

Artist: Kate Bush   Features in: Season 4

'Running Up That Hill' plays as Max battles Vecna in the Upside Down. The boys scramble to find the right cassette to put in her Walkman to break Max out of her hypnotic state, as the world held its breath. An epic tune for an epic scene, Absolute goosebumps.

DO YOU AGREE WITH US, OR WOULD YOU CHOOSE DIFFERENT SONGS? FILL IN YOUR OWN TOP 10 HERE!

#1 SONG TITLE: ....

#2 SONG TITLE: ....

#3 SONG TITLE: ....

#4 SONG TITLE: ....

#5 SONG TITLE: ....

#6 SONG TITLE: ....

#7 SONG TITLE: ....

#8 SONG TITLE: ....

#9 SONG TITLE: ....

#10 SONG TITLE: ....

WHICH STRANGER THINGS CHARACTER ARE YOU?

We know the characters inside out (and upside down) – but which member of the *Stranger Things* gang are YOU most like? Take our fabulous quiz to find out once and for all!

WHAT'S YOUR FAVOURITE FILM?

A - *Lord of The Rings*

B - *E.T.*

C - *Karate Kid*

D - *Never Ending Story*

E - *How the Grinch Stole Christmas*

F - *The Shawshank Redemption*

WHAT'S YOUR FAVOURITE HOBBY?

A - Fantasy roleplaying

B - Hanging out with your best friend

C - Skateboarding

D - Taking things apart to see how they work

E - Playing basketball

F - Spending time with your partner

WHERE'S YOUR FAVOURITE PLACE TO HANG OUT?

A - In your own private den

B - At a science fair

C - At a big shopping mall

D - Your local arcade

E - At your local sports park

F - Outside in nature

WHAT WORD WOULD YOUR FRIENDS USE TO BEST DESCRIBE YOU?

A - Honest

B - Leader

C - Determined

D - Funny

E - Clever

F - Loyal

IF YOU COULD ONLY EAT/DRINK ONE THING FOR THE REST OF YOUR LIFE, WHAT WOULD IT BE?

A - Anything home cooked by your mum

B - Pineapple pizza

C - Ice cream

D - Bologna sandwiches

E - New Coke

F - Eggos

WHAT IS YOUR DREAM JOB?

A - Comic book artist
B - Writer
C - Pro skateboarder
D - Cryptozoologist
E - Sports star
F - Social worker

WHO IS YOUR HERO?

A - Stan Lee
B - Albert Einstein
C - Tony Hawk
D - Steve Harrington
E - Kobe Bryant
F - Dynamo

IF YOU HAD A SUPERPOWER, WHAT WOULD IT BE?

A - Invisibility
B - Shapeshifter
C - None, superpowers are so overrated!
D - Time travel
E - Superspeed
F - Telekinesis

YOU'RE AT SCOOPS AHOY AND YOU ASK TO SAMPLE SOME ICE CREAM. WHAT FLAVOUR DO YOU ASK FOR?

A - Strawberry
B - Cookie dough
C - Mint choc chip
D - Bubble gum
E - Salted caramel
F - Rocky road

YOU JUST ARRIVED AT STARCOURT MALL. WHERE DO YOU HEAD FIRST?

A - The exit, mall's are not my thing!
B - The cinema
C - The arcade
D - Ice cream parlour
E - Sports shop
F - Your favourite clothes shop

IF YOU ANSWERED...

MOSTLY As

You're Will!
A quiet introvert who enjoys the simple pleasures in life.

MOSTLY Bs

You're Mike!
A leader by nature, with a ferocious intellect and thirst for knowledge.

MOSTLY Cs

You're Max!
An active, fun loving type who knows what they want from life and won't be messed around!

MOSTLY Ds

You're Dustin!
A loveable nerd with an appetite for curiousity!

MOSTLY Es

You're Lucas!
You can hang with nerds but still rock it with the cool kids- not forgetting your roots though!

MOSTLY Fs

You're Eleven!
A loyal, brave person who will do anything for their friends!

ARE YOU A SUPERFAN?

SEASON ONE

1
What 3 letter word did the Christmas lights spell out to Joyce?

2
What was the name of the diner Eleven walks in to in the very first episode?

3
Who's house was Barb at when she disappeared?

4
Out of all the main *Stranger Things* characters, who appears first in episode one?

5
Mike nearly jumps in to which quarry before El saves him with her powers?

6
What is the name of Will's den in the woods at the back of his home?

7
What comic does Will want from Dustin after winning the bike race?

8
What does Hopper find when he cuts open 'Wills' body?

9
What weapon does Lucas use to fight the Demogorgan?

10
What is the name of the science teacher the boys look up to?

40 questions across each season stand between you and *Stranger Things* Superfan status! If you find it tough, don't worry, all the answers can be found in the pages of this book, so make sure you've read it all before you tackle this superquiz! Test your friends and see who can score the highest – but be careful, the loser might be banished to the Upside Down!

SEE PAGE 78 FOR THE ANSWERS!
NO CHEATING!

SEASON TWO

11
What is the name Max uses on the arcade machine leaderboards?

12
Which city does Eleven travel to so she can meet Kali?

13
What number is Eleven's sister Kali?

14
What's the full name that Dustin gave to his pet Demodog?

15
Which store did Bob Newby work at?

16
What do the boys dress up as at Halloween?

17
What song do Eleven and Mike dance to at the Snow Ball?

18
What is the surname of Max's brother Billy?

19
Who dances with Lucas at the Snow Ball?

20
What is the name given to the monster Eleven battles with in the season finale?

SEASON THREE

21

What is the name of Dustin's girlfriend?

22

On Robin's chart, how many 'You Suck' marks has Steve got?

23

What is the name of the shopping mall?

24

Who are the two mind flayed characters Nancy and Jonathan battle with at the Hawkins Memorial Hospital?

25

How many inches does Hopper say Eleven's bedroom door must be open when Mike is there?

26

In Season 3, Where do Steve and Robin work?

27

Who is Robin's High School crush?

28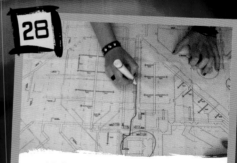

Who ends up crawling through the air vents at the mall?

29

When Dustin sings a duet with his girlfriend, what song do they sing?

30

Who gets sprayed in the face when the gang surprise Dustin?

SEASON FOUR

31 Which famous horror movie actor plays Victor Creel?

32 What number did Henry Creel (Vecna) reveal to be?

33 What topping does Argyle love to put on his pizza?

34 'Master of _____' is the epic tune Eddie rocks on the guitar.

35 What is the name of the Russian prison camp, Hopper was a prisoner at?

36 What number basketball shirt does Lucas wear?

37 Who was Vecna's first victim?

38 Where do Steve and Robin work in Season 4?

39 Who takes Eleven to the Nina Project?

40 What song saves Max from Vecna?

STRANGER THINGS

What happens next?

Ok, so this kind of thing might be easy for someone with special powers like Eleven, but that doesn't mean us mere mortals can't try to predict what the Duffer brothers have up their sleeves for us when Season 5 finally lands. Here are some of the more interesting theories...

ZOMBIE MOVIE

Maybe Vecna has kept all his victims alive in the Upside Down – after all, he was able to survive there for years. He will open another gate and bring them back as a wave of attackers, perhaps operating like a hive mind as the Mind Flayed did in Season 3.

EDDIE RETURNS

Eddie was hugely popular, and there have been online petitions to bring him back. IT's possible he might return as a half human, half demon but with good intentions to help defeat Vecna. Please, please, please be true!!

WILL THE POWERFUL

Having spent quite some time in the Upside Down, it's possible that Will acquired powers of his own – possibly even stronger than Eleven's – but hasn't realised it yet. He could end up fighting alongside El to destroy the Upside Down – or his power might turn him into another Vecna and the team need to defeat him!

IT'S ONLY A GAME

There's a popular fan theory that everything is happening inside a game of D&D that Will is running. None of it has really happened, and it's all just a quest he has invented. The theory is that he is manipulating everything that happens – there are certainly strong similarities between the series and the D&D game that Will runs within it.

 001   **011**

SHE SAID YES!

They've been through such a lot, it feels kind of fated that they should tie the knot at the end of Season 5, doesn't it? Eleven could be a bridesmaid and Murray could be best man. It would be epic...

ELEVEN DIES

She has willingly sacrificed herself before, surviving when she honestly believed she would die ('Goodbye, Mike' remember?). There's a chance that the only way to close the gate permanently and cut the link between our world and the Upside Down would require so much of her mental energy that it destroys her? We hope not, but we know that El is brave enough to do it...

What do you think will happen in Season 5?

Who will be the biggest hero? ....

Most shocking moment/death? ....

Nancy ends up with... JONATHAN ☐ STEVE ☐ NO ONE ☐

Eddie returns? YES ☐ No ☐   Does Will get powers? YES ☐ No ☐

ANSWERS

16-17 TRUE OR FALSE

1 True
2 False, she was the eleventh child to join the programme
3 False, they were nicknamed 'The Tigers'
4 True
5 False, they moved from California
6 False, Hawkins Indiana is a fictional town
7 False, he had a daughter called Sarah
8 True
9 False, Will plays as a Wizard
10 False, she's called Erika
11 True
12 False, Will is the first to dissapear
13 True
14 False, Bob was manager of RadioShack

46 WORDSEARCH

D	P	T	C	P	N	Y	U	W	L	V	I	O	A	H
X	U	E	P	A	L	A	C	E	E	I	J	N	A	M
S	D	S	H	B	D	R	O	C	J	T	A	W	J	I
R	W	D	T	L	X	W	N	F	K	I	K	Y	S	N
U	W	N	S	I	L	A	T	X	D	I	C	O	H	D
P	R	S	C	R	N	I	R	N	N	T	I	H	O	F
S	H	J	A	E	E	N	I	S	J	X	U	A	P	L
I	G	G	R	C	E	Y	E	G	G	O	S	S	P	A
D	F	E	T	V	U	K	B	M	E	M	N	P	E	Y
E	F	B	E	F	H	L	J	X	D	D	S	O	R	E
D	X	L	B	R	E	N	N	E	R	D	A	O	N	R
O	E	H	U	K	K	S	V	P	A	I	J	C	U	U
W	N	O	G	R	O	G	O	M	E	D	W	S	R	F
N	O	T	E	L	E	K	E	N	I	S	I	S	N	A
L	P	P	J	A	C	B	M	D	F	F	O	Q	M	M

47 CROSSWORD

Down
1 Vecna
2 Sinclair
4 Noah Schnapp
5 Hellfire Club
6 Chief of Police
7 Eggos
10 Eleven
11 California
13 Indiana
16 Max

Across
3 Dungeons
8 The Palace
9 Swimming Pool
12 Master Of Puppets
14 Upside Down
15 Right Here
17 D'artagnan

72-75 ARE YOU A SUPERFAN?

Season One
1 RUN
2 Benny's Diner
3 Steve's
4 Mike
5 Sattler's Quarry
6 Castle Byers
7 X-Men #134
8 Cotton Wool
9 Slingshot
10 Mr Clarke

Season Two
11 MADMAX
12 Chicago
13 Eight (008)
14 D'artagnan
15 RadioShack
16 Ghostbusters
17 Every Breath You Take
18 Hargrove
19 Max
20 Mind Flayer

Season Three
21 Suzie
22 Six
23 Starcourt Mall
24 Tom and Bruce
25 Three inches
26 Scoops Ahoy
27 Tammy Thompson
28 Erika
29 Never Ending Story
30 Lucas

Season Four
31 Robert Englund
32 One (001)
33 Pineappple
34 Puppets
35 Kamchatka
36 Number 8
37 Chrissy
38 Family Video
39 Dr Owens
40 Running Up That Hill